A PLANET OF GRACE

A PLANET OF GRACE

Images and Words from Biosphere One

Written by Bernadette McCarver Snyder
Photographs and Foreword by James Stephen Behrens, OCSO

acta
PUBLICATIONS

A PLANET OF GRACE
Images and Words from Biosphere One
Written by Bernadette McCarver Snyder
Photographs and Foreword by James Stephen Behrens, OCSO

Edited by Paul Pennick and L.C. Fiore
Cover Design by Tom A. Wright
Text design, typesetting and photographs on pages 33, 35, 43, 44, 48, 76 and 91 by Patricia A. Lynch

Scripture quotations contained herein are from the *New Revised Standard Version Bible*, copyright ©1989 by the Division of Christian Education of the National Council of the Churches of Christ in the U.S.A. Used by permission. All rights reserved.

Copyright © 2009 by Bernadette McCarver Snyder and James Stephen Behrens, OCSO

Published by ACTA Publications, 5559 W. Howard St., Skokie, IL 60077
(800) 397-2282, www.actapublications.com

Library of Congress Control Number: 2007927590
ISBN: 978-0-87946-401-1
Printed in Canada for Graphics TwoFortyFour, Inc.
Year: 15 14 13 12 11 10 09
Printing: 10 9 8 7 6 5 4 3 2 First Edition

♻ Text printed on 10% post-consumer waste recycled paper.

If you only knock long enough…
you are sure to wake up someone.

Henry Wadsworth Longfellow

I dedicate this book to all who have knocked
and all who did—or will—wake up.

And I gratefully dedicate it to Paul Pennick,
great editor, good friend,
who can light up any environment
and encouraged me to write this book.

FOREWORD

Near the small church where I once served as a parish priest, there was a revival. It was held in a tent on a large, dirt lot. The tent rose each year, and people came to sing and clap and rock to the wonderful gospel music. Human spirits rose too: A revival is all about recharging one's heart for the rest of the year until the tent returns with all its wonders.

You have in your hands an invitation to partake in a different, but no less wondrous, kind of revival. In the pages that follow, Bernadette McCarver Snyder's words plead for renewal—of the ways we see our world and learn to care for it. You do not need a ticket, and no tent is expected to rise. The lot where the revival needs to take place is the soil of life, our planet, and *A Planet of Grace* is a primer in learning how to look about and see, find and do. Inside this book is a wealth of examples of how a remarkable writer sees the world around her, as dry and troubled as it is, and goes about doing what she can to become a hands-on ecologist. As she is careful to note, we are all too ready to be bowled over by the enormity of the problem and too tempted to leave the work to the experts.

But the experts are pointing in our direction. They are more than willing to teach us how to heal our planet.

Bernadette also shares her own expertise in this book. You may be gazing out a window, wondering where to begin. Look no further. As you turn each page, you will find remarkable examples of how to start right where you live. Bernadette writes of gardening and of capturing the light of the sun for power in something as common as a Mason jar. She has trained her eye and her memory to see the small world about her for all its possibilities.

In one essay, she writes of a use we have found for sand. Silicon possesses remarkable power—if harnessed properly. We walk on it every day. It is all over the earth, in abundance. When the need came, we turned to it for electronics and computers.

In another essay, she writes of birds called Booby Birds. They wrap their large blue feet around their yet-to-be hatched eggs. From such secure warmth, the eggs grow and then are hatched.

Our planet is begging for revival. It needs a daily tent-raising—it needs the song of your active engagement for its health. Wrap your hands and heart around this book and learn the secrets of your immediate surroundings—the many ordinary ways you can heal our wounded Earth and find comfort in its healing. Ours is a world waiting to be hatched.

James Stephen Behrens, OCSO
Monastery of the Holy Spirit
Conyers, Georgia

INTRODUCTION

Your careless gifts of a moment,
like the meteors of an autumn night,
catch fire in the depth of my being.

R. Tagore

Oh yes. In the depth of my being, I have rejoiced in the way God spreads his gifts generously and freely—for all to notice, cherish and protect in this multi-splendored planet of ours. However, I never associated the word *careless* with his presents or presence until I read this quote. As I love Tagore's nature poems, I know this famous Eastern mystic and Western educator must have used that word to mean "unstudied, spontaneous." And I love the idea of God spontaneously showering us with gifts on an autumn night.

Just yesterday, I was reminded of this while eating lunch outdoors on a surprisingly cool summer afternoon. A small—possibly teenaged—grasshopper suddenly appeared on my table. Because it was lunchtime, I edged a bit of lettuce in his direction. He checked it out with his long feelers and then settled down to munch as I munched on my sandwich.

When I myself was a teenager, wandering far afield looking for new adventures, I would have reacted to a grasshopper near my lunch with a squeal as I tried to shoo it as far away from me as possible. I might have even stomped on it. And yes, I still swat at those pesky mosquitoes and flies that sometimes enter my home uninvited. But yesterday, the small grasshopper seemed like a gift, a reminder of how vulnerable so many of God's wonders, great and small, are today—from oceans and glaciers to songbirds and bumblebees.

We live on a blessed, beautiful but endangered planet—often unaware, ungrateful. And I ashamedly admit that I have been one of the lazy stewards. Now I begin to realize the need to reverence all of God's mind-boggling creations—to first see, and then appreciate, and then protect.

Belatedly, the media and some businesses have become aware of the need to address environmental problems. But as they publicize the "greening" movement and refer to those who work to make a difference as *ecocentric* or *ecomaniacs*, they make stewardship sound like a passing fad: to be acknowledged, but only as an observer, not a participant.

Saving our home planet is not a spectator sport. It may seem audacious to think that one person can really make a difference—just one person, reaching out. But that's the way every invention, discovery, exploration and redemption has begun—with one person, seeing and reaching out.

Today as I wander through my own small corner of earth, I am newly grateful that I am so often gifted with sights and scenes that make me stop and pay attention. And I invite you to wander with me—to see the surprising ways others are meeting the stewardship challenge, one person at a time. And to thank God for the many gifts and joys he has entrusted to us on this, our blessed planet earth.

Bernadette McCarver Snyder
St. Louis, Missouri

When we tug on a single thing in nature, we find it attached to everything else.

John Muir

Glimpsing bare-branched trees standing bravely together, yet looking lonely and abandoned, has always made me feel melancholy—until today. Today they seemed like guardians: holding the fort, protecting their part of the planet until spring. Without the camouflage of leaves, they also seemed to be daring me to see each individual tree apart from the group, to see each tree's strength, endurance and value without veneer or decoration. I noticed the rugged bark, the graceful bending of each limb, the unique way the years had shaped each tree a bit differently. The starkness of their simplicity allowed me to see through the crowd and beyond, to new vistas and opportunities.

Dear Lord, remind me to look beyond the world's camouflage so I can appreciate the value and uniqueness of your creations. Forgive me if I sometimes hide behind my own camouflage, because I'm not always brave enough to put my best branch forward without any decoration. But I'm trying, Lord. I'm trying.

The pinecone tree in my front yard is shaped like a lacy umbrella that somebody used to fend off a burglar. Its twisted staves and branches droop unashamedly on one side, while the other side spreads out jauntily. I call it my Resurrection Tree. Every year a few limbs dry up and fall off, and I think the end is near. But no: It reaches out with new, lacy but uncoordinated limbs and continues to produce a carpet of pinecones. Other people make lovely wreaths and decorations from pinecones, so I package mine up and give them to those other people. But I love the spunk of this tree. I check on it regularly, carting away the broken bits and pieces, gently patting its trunk (because I'm afraid a good shove would knock it down), and using it as a role model for my own broken bits and pieces.

Dear Lord, give me the gumption of that imperfect, lacy umbrella. When I am tempted to give in or give up, stick a pinecone in my ear and whisper, "Resurrection." I know there are many forlorn places on the earth that would welcome the meager shade of even one lopsided tree. Bless them, Lord. Send them rain for their crops, seed for their tomorrows, and a Resurrection harvest.

My friend can look out her kitchen window and see a flock of tiny yellow birds that visit her birdfeeders regularly. My sister once had two hummingbird feeders outside her kitchen window, and she watched the hummers who frequently stopped by for a snack. So I purchased a new birdfeeder and filled it with yellow-bird food. I hung up a hummingbird feeder filled with bright-red, sugary liquid. I sent out the invitations…but nobody came. It's okay though, because yellow butterflies visit my flowers, and redbirds and blue jays and mockingbirds take splashy dips and drink from my birdbaths. The wonders of nature: Best-made plans go awry, but unplanned blessings arrive every day.

Dear Lord, as a special joy for me, a tiny wren moved into the old, scraggy birdhouse that's been hanging in the holly tree for years—totally ignoring the brand new, beautiful bird domicile I thought a fine-feathered friend would appreciate. He serenades me every day and I love it, but I don't think he means it as a serenade. I think he's really singing, "Bye, bye, lady, this space is my place. So go, go, go away from my patio!" Speaking of unplanned-ness, Lord, forgive us for not seeing the need sooner for plans to protect your surprising world. I pray that new plans and new work will be in time to save the birdsong and all the surprising glories of your planet.

The uncertain glory of an April day.

Shakespeare

There's a tiny, green iris in my eye and a frilly, purple iris flower in my garden. I know a lady who was named Iris in honor of the Greek Goddess, and I've seen a multi-colored rainbow in the sky…which is also known as an iris. All of these irises are spectacular, but when I was growing up in Tennessee, I walked to school past a field which regularly burst forth with hundreds of spectacular iris blossoms of many colors and frills—and locally they were simply called "flags." As the state flower of Tennessee, they should have flagged our attention, but they grew in such profusion that no one noticed them much. Today, I see them as a country cousin to the exotic orchid, and revel in the colorful variety of their fancy, frilly petals.

Dear Lord, thank you for the sturdy plants who seem to flourish with little need for care, and for the frail plants who struggle bravely, reminding us how fragile life is and of our need to protect it. And Lord, I'm sorry I forgot to water my tiny patio garden last night. I'll do it right now. I promise.

May the sun bring you new energy by day,
may the moon softly restore you by night,
may the rain wash away your worries,
may the breeze blow new strength
 into your being.
May you walk gently through the world
and know its beauty all the days of your life.

Apache blessing

God created the world; I do him no wrong if I want to enjoy it.

Blessed Hildegard of Bingen

One year, on vacation, we had fun at a restaurant that had a thatched roof. There were little goats on the roof that enjoyed their lunch as we enjoyed ours. I smiled recently when I read that in cities across the country, rooftops of tall buildings are now being carpeted with wildflowers, sedums or grasses. These "eco-roofs" soak up storm water, help prevent flooding, save energy by cooling buildings and cities, and provide habitat for birds, butterflies and other high-flying wildlife. In Chicago, where summers sizzle and winters are wild, City Hall has been retro-fitted with a green roof like a prairie. Another city is installing eco-roofs on all new city-owned buildings, where feasible, hoping reduced runoff from intense storms will save millions by eliminating the need for more sewer pipes and sewer plant capacity. Planting these rooftop gardens has taken a lot of research and extensive work with architects and roofing contractors. So don't try this at home—unless you're ready for the roof to fall in!

Dear Lord, I always dreamed that some day I would live in a penthouse with a few potted plants on my rooftop patio. I would wear a designer outfit and look down on the peasants below. Instead, I live in a standard subdivision with a patio surrounded by unruly plants, cheery flowers, and crazy birds that look down on me as I dig around in my dirty dungarees. And I love it. Thank you, Lord, for friendly backyards and for forward-looking city planners with their earth-friendly, decorated roofs.

I'm always surprised that God chose an apple as the ultimate temptation, when surely it should have been a summer-ripe, homegrown, red-juicy tomato. My love of tomatoes began with the ones my mother grew outside our backdoor, in a tiny plot of what must have been the richest garden soil since Eden. Her tomatoes were the best ever. Some years later, in a new town with a new life, my husband and ten-year-old son and I moved to a new house toward the end of summer. We inherited a nice, little garden the former owners had planted. At last, I once again could pick homegrown tomatoes from my own backyard—until the frost came. By the next summer, I had a new job and little time for gardening. But I soon found a small farm where I could stop after work and bring home bargain-priced bags of sinfully-red, ripe homegrowns. When I left that job, I hated to leave my friends and co-workers, but I really missed the farmer and his tomatoes.

Dear Lord, others seek gold and treasure, but every summer I seek tomatoes. I had finally found a different farmer who repaired lawn mowers and sold warm, just-picked tomatoes. But this year, I hurried to his out-of-the-way patch of earth, and there were no lawn mowers and no tomatoes. Now, grocery tomatoes look good but never taste right. Is that because backyard gardens are more like Eden—ecologically correct instead of politically correct…and no preservatives? Is that why tomatoes were once known as "love apples?"

I have sometimes been accused of going around in circles when I shop, deliver, pick up, drop off, and so forth in my daily travels. Now I find that going around in circles is energy efficient. A major delivery company redesigned its routes so its drivers would seldom have to make left-hand turns. Amazingly, making only right turns cut 30 million miles off deliveries in a single year, and saved three million gallons of gas. Why? Turning right means cars and trucks don't have to idle, burning fuel and releasing emissions, while waiting for a chance to go left across oncoming traffic—which means right turns are also safer. Who knew going right could be so…right?

Dear Lord, those professional drivers know where they're going, but I don't have a well-designed route or a decent sense of direction. Turning right instead of left could get me hopelessly lost in a subdivision or right back where I started. However, this does teach me that making one small change in a driving habit (or any habit) could turn into a financial, environmental or spiritual benefit. People like me can't make a big difference to save the planet, but we can help by making small changes. Right?

Yes, I do. I admit it. I talk to my plants and flowers. And they nod their pretty little heads and cheer me up with their go-greenness. But there is one plant that really should be listed on my family tree. Actually, it is pictured in my family album: There's the photo of my grandfather looking very sophisticated with his bushy mustache, wearing his best suit and tie, a flower in his buttonhole—and his elephant ears jutting out on each side of his handsome face. There are similar photos of my father, uncles, cousins, and assorted male relatives—all wearing faces decorated with those elephant-sized ears. Most of the female relatives evidently learned early, as I did, to find a hairdo long enough to cover up the family trademark. They appear in the photograph album in disguise.

Dear Lord, the Elephant Ear plant family adds a lot of green wherever it grows. Help my family and all families—with ears large or small—to tune into the greening message. Help us take a little extra time to recycle, rethink our priorities, revise our lifestyles, resolve to make big changes, and never relax in our dedication. And if we manage to do all those things, Lord, you can rejoice in the miracle.

I was daydreaming and skywalking today, watching a procession of puffy white clouds meander across the sky above my backyard. When I was in school, I surely learned the names of all the different kinds of clouds, but I couldn't remember any today except thunder clouds (the kind I often see in my mirror). I decided to drag out the encyclopedia and look them up. Wow! Maybe I never did know all their exotic names: Nimbostratus, Cirrocumulus, Cumulonimbus, Altostratus. I vaguely recall the name Cirrus and the puffy, white Cumulus...and I remember lying in the grass, picking out the clouds that looked like a castle, or a monkey riding on an elephant, or a monster shooting lightning bolts. (I knew to run from that last one.) I really should try to learn those proper meteorological names, because I spend so much time with my head in the clouds.

Dear Lord, today those puffy clouds reminded me of the cotton candy at the county fair, whipped cream on an ice cream sundae, and piles of homemade mashed potatoes. Yes, you guessed it, Lord—I'm on a diet again. I should be thinking of the whiteness of a baptismal gown, creamy white candles, a bride's lovely dress, and gardenias. I should be thinking of white sandy beaches cleared of the trash left by sunbathers, white ocean waves cleared of oil spills, white downtown buildings without graffiti, white consciences free of coulda-but-didn'ts. Is that just dreaming too? I pray not.

God saw everything that he had made,
And, indeed, it was very good.

Genesis 1:31

Oh no! I just heard that our beautiful Pacific Ocean is being threatened by something similar to that cult-classic horror movie, *The Blob*. The movie is about a strange "ooze" that devours the inhabitants of a ski resort. I was too squeamish to ever see the movie, but I couldn't help but think of it today when an Internet story described a huge blob of plastic trash, double the size of the continental United States, floating in the Pacific Ocean. It seems that dangerous chemicals from industrial waste, which also seep into the ocean, stick to the plastic and are ingested by marine life, birds and, through the food chain, possibly humans. I don't know where the movie blob came from, but this plastic blob came from rivers, boats, beaches—and people. I hope experts are working to clean up our ocean blobs, but right now I don't even want to go into my kitchen. I know there are a couple of scary plastic bags in there, left over from my recent shopping trip. Shame on me.

Dear Lord, remind me to get out the cloth bags for my next shopping spree. I hear that some countries are beginning to outlaw non-recyclable plastic bags. Help that practice to spread, Lord—faster than the blobs are spreading in our waterways. We were blessed with the water of baptism. Help us be alert and aware of how precious your ocean water is.

How sweet it is! Years ago, doctors discovered the healing properties of honey. But then came modern wonder drugs. Now, as some bacteria have become increasingly resistant to antibiotics, doctors are rediscovering this sweet, old healer. For several years the burn and wound sections of hospitals in Asia and Europe have been using bandages infused with powerful honey from the manuka trees in New Zealand. It seems that honey fights bacteria in many ways, including the steady production of the antiseptic hydrogen peroxide. Now U. S. and Canadian hospitals are trying this old-new treatment. Unfortunately, this is happening just when honey and honeybees are becoming scarce. For several years, I took kids to a nearby farm where the farmer had put a bee colony and hive between two sturdy pieces of glass. The kids were fascinated by the bees busily at work. This year I went back and the bees were gone. The farmer said they left and didn't return. Let's hope there will still be plenty of busy bees in New Zealand.

Dear Lord, you've put so many healing secrets in nature—like the many medicines that come from plants in the rain forest. Thank you for letting wise scientists discover your secrets—from wonder drugs to honey. Please Lord, keep those New Zealand bees safe, and please send more honeybees buzzing back into our honey-hungry world.

You shine into my soul like the sun against gold. When I may rest in you, Lord, my joy is rich.

Mechtild of Magdeberg

One of the few riddles I remember from my distant childhood was the one that asked, "What is black and white and read all over?" Of course, it was the newspaper. Today you can ask what is black and white and green all over, because some newspapers are now using earth-friendly, vegetable-based soy ink in their newspaper printing. Not only is the soy ink more environmentally-friendly than petroleum-based ink, it is also available in brighter colors, can improve the lifespan of printers, and makes it easier to recycle the paper. Of course, all newspapers are different in their distribution, printing presses, and other machinery, so they can't all use this new ink. But many are trying. The soy-inked newspapers are also great for plants, especially if used for compost. Or you can just lay these used newspapers around your plants and cover them with mulch to keep weeds at a minimum. What a great new "soy sauce" discovery!

Dear Lord, I love computers. But it's no fun trying to read the daily newspaper on a little square at your desk. I want something I can fold up, stick under my arm, and take with me to the patio, a park bench, or anywhere I have to go where I will be "kept waiting"—and there are a lot of those places. Until some terrible person decides to do away with all newspapers, I still can keep up on the worldwide news, work the crossword puzzle, giggle at the comics, put the paper in a recycling bin, and see how easy it can be going green.

If seeds in the black earth can turn into such beautiful roses,
what might the heart of man become in its long journey to the stars?

Gilbert Chesterton

Once kids get a chance to get out in it, they usually love the earth. They must, because they drag so much of it back into the house with them. But sometimes I worry that our children hear so much about the environmental problems they might get discouraged about the future world that belongs to them. Then today a friend told me about her child's class project. They were to design a city of the future. The kids designed a city with lots of solar panels, green spaces, moving sidewalks, recycling centers, community vegetable gardens, hybrid cars, etc. They had heard the message and were immediately putting the information to work. They weren't depressed or hopeless or ready to give up on the planet the way a lot of adults are. They were having a ball thinking up practical—and a few outlandish—ideas for their future. Maybe it's true: A little child shall lead them.

Dear Lord, remind us to not be too negative when we talk to kids about environmental problems. We need to encourage their faith in the future, applaud their joy and creativity, so they see possibilities when we see impossibilities. Help us to instill in them a sense of wonder that will grow and stay with them the rest of their lives. Help us allow them to have fun and dream dreams of an interesting future for this amazing home planet you gave them.

In ancient Egypt, some believed the dead would be asked three questions before they could cross into the afterlife: "Did you lie? Did you steal? Did you pollute the Nile?" Oh my. If that still happens, I may be in a lot of trouble. I never told an out-and-out lie unless it was absolutely necessary… but I have been known to embroider the facts. And I never really stole any one thing, but as a writer, I often quote others, which could count as stealing their words or ideas. And although I would love to travel and see the Nile, I never have. So I might be in the clear there, unless that question has been modernized to include other types of pollution. I have probably helped pollute the air, the earth, the rivers, without even realizing it. Oh my. The sin of omission hangs heavy o'er my head.

Dear Lord, many of us would have loved to save the earth by not polluting it long before now, if we had only realized what was happening. But with all those corners to dust, appointments to keep, gardens to dig, and dreams to dream about visiting the Nile, we just let it fall off our radar. I know that's not a very good excuse, but what's a person to do? I know. I know. A person should get busy and make up for lost time.

They say it's important to have a friendly approach to your home, so my husband and I spent good money to install a pretty, pebbly-looking sidewalk leading to a pebbly-looking front porch. But now the sidewalk has a small crack in it where *someone* let the lawnmower blade take a bite out. I know I'll have to have it repaired one day, but having a cracked approach to our home seems appropriate. And it offers many possibilities for meditation. We must consider all our bad habits that need repair. We can think how our daily worries and frustrations are small as pebbles compared to others in the wide world. We can be grateful that we have a sidewalk and a house instead of a gravel path and a thatched hut. And we can feel guilty knowing that many who live in huts or cardboard boxes may be kinder than we are, care more for fellow-sufferers than we do, or pray more often or more effectively than we pray.

Dear Lord, you notice I keep saying "we," but you and I know it should be singular. I am grateful for my sidewalk and house, but I know I should take more than pebble-sized times for prayer in my busy days. I should be more aware of the plights of others and more attuned to the suffering world at large. Thank you, Lord, for showing me pebbles and possibilities.

People are like stained-glass windows. They sparkle and shine when the sun is out,
but when the darkness sets in, their true beauty is revealed only if there is a light from within.

Elizabeth Kübler-Ross

My recipe box is like an old photograph album. When I search through it, looking for a supper idea, I see all my relatives. I find recipes from mama, grandma, Aunt Linnie, cousin Annie Laurie, my sister (in her beautiful handwriting telling me where she was when she got this recipe from a friend or neighbor), and the secret for Aunt Iva's Cold Oven Poundcake. I'm always clipping out new recipes to add to the old, but recently I've found a different kind of recipe—with ingredients such as baking soda, baker's yeast, white chalk, liquid soap, and cedar chips. They're all "recipes" for less-toxic alternatives to cleaning with hazardous household chemicals. They promise improved indoor air, less waste disposal, and less cost. Some of my oldest recipes include some strange old-time ingredients, but none of them include chalk, soap or cedar chips. These family recipes do, however, improve the indoor air because, while they are cooking, the whole house fills with delicious aromas.

Dear Lord, I suspect that some of these "new" recipes for cleaning up the home environment are really old ones our foremothers used, because they didn't have a grocery store with an entire aisle full of "new and improved" cleaning solutions handily stored in spray cans. Thank you for our creative ancestors who made do with whatever they had, and thank you for those who are reminding us to return to some of those old, homemade recipes.

Contentment is not the fulfillment of what you want,
but the realization of how much you already have.

Anon

My worry list contains a strange assortment of things that crowd my brain, but the word *glacier* never appeared there—probably because there isn't a single glacier in my entire neighborhood. Then today I heard a radio show about the glaciers in a small area of South America. Someone compared the glaciers to a savings account. In winter, snow piles up, accumulating ice deposits instead of interest. When warmer weather arrives, the glaciers melt, allowing the villagers to make "withdrawals" of water for drinking and bathing, to water their crops, wash their clothes, etc. Recently the glaciers began to "gain interest," because they started melting too much. The villagers suddenly had to imagine what would happen if their savings accounts ran out. Without those life-saving withdrawals, they might be forced to leave their homes, abandon their villages, and seek water somewhere else. It was time to worry.

Dear Lord, I do know about having a savings account that becomes depleted with little hope of bringing it back. But in all these years I was never concerned about villagers who depended on a neighborhood-savings-account glacier to support the lifestyle to which they had become accustomed. Too late I came to sympathize, empathize and pray for them. Every time I turn on the tap in the kitchen, Lord, remind me to pray for those who have needs so different from my own. Remind me that we all share this one planet, this one family.

Tonight while slicing fresh mushrooms into spaghetti sauce, I remembered an amazing trivia fact. According to researchers, the largest living thing, the world's single biggest organism, is a mushroom. It's a fungus like you might see anywhere growing on a dead tree stump. But this fungus is several thousand years old and covers 2,200 acres in the Malheur National Forest in Oregon. It grows mostly underground, spreading along tree roots, sometimes poking out of the soil as a little clump of honey mushrooms—but each clump is connected and continuing to grow and spread. I sometimes feel like that after a big serving of mushroom-sauce spaghetti (spread out and continuing to spread), but who would have suspected that I was connected with a huge mushroom family living a secret underground life in Oregon?

Dear Lord, this mushroom story should be a good way to remember how we are all connected, across the world. We pop up here and there, but we are all responsible for the future life of our planet. Teach us, Lord, to stay connected and work to save the many living things in our world—both great and small.

Help! I'm a captive! Frozen in my daily rut, I hang here, waiting for something or someone to come along and set me free. To be honest, I know that's not going to happen. But unlike Little Oprhan Annie, I don't have to wait for the sun to come out tomorrow. God's sun is shining now, sending the warmth of faith to gradually defrost my outer shell, to melt my indecision, to help me be a new me—or even a little-bit-new me. I'm slowly getting the message, because from my window I can see what's happening outside—shrubs casting aside their shawls of snow, tree branches weeping away their worries, tiny green shoots nosing their way through the frozen earth, reaching for the sun. While I'm in my cozy kitchen, they're all out in the cold, bravely trying to show me the way.

Dear Lord, thank you for always sending me a message when I need one. You know that I don't really want to break totally free. I know I am needed in my rut, but I also know there is still room to go forth, discover, learn and enjoy. Your planet earth can guide me.

The world is but canvas to our imaginations.

Henry David Thoreau

In my perambulations near and far, I have never spotted a Sandhill Crane. Evidently that's because I've never been to Nebraska or stopped by the banks of the Platte River. I just learned that a stretch of the Platte is an ancient oasis for these long-necked cranes that travel up the central flyway. Each spring more than half a million gather there to rest and refuel and find safe nighttime roosts before journeying on to northern breeding grounds. Although I've never seen one, I can identify with them because I too have often looked for a safe nighttime roost. I know how good it is to finally settle down at a friendly inn that offers comfy beds and warm breakfasts.

Dear Lord, although I've never seen many of the endangered people or plants or animals on our complex planet, I can identify with them because we share the same need for food, rest and safety. Although my friends and I try to recycle, send money, and pray for the endangered, we feel helpless in the face of such great need. You, Lord, needed only a bit of bread and a few fishes to feed a multitude, but we know we can't work miracles like that. Help us to do what we can, whenever and wherever we can. Help us trust in you to turn our measly bits into miracles.

Did you know that Antarctica is the driest place on earth— and also the wettest? The Sahara desert receives only one inch of rain per year. In the area known as the Dry Valleys of Antarctic, it never rains at all. Yet Antarctica is also the wettest continent on earth because other parts of this continent contain 70 percent of the world's fresh water…in the form of ice. I suppose all of our continents are full of contradictions— the rich and poor, the workers and the shirkers, the recyclers who collect every aluminum can but have three gas-guzzlers in their driveway. And then there's the ultimate in contradictions, found on every planet—teenagers. But that's another story.

Dear Lord, to be honest, my prayer life is a contradiction too. Some days it can be as dry as a desert. Other days, I am so full of faith and praise and hope and thanksgiving that I might break into tears of joy. I never realized before that I had so much in common with the continents, although I should have when my middle-aged middle turned into a continental drift! Oh well, thank you, Lord, for the dry times that teach us to appreciate refreshing rain. Thank you for teenagers and for recyclers. Save us all.

Growing up in the South, I became familiar with Mason jars. I saw them sitting on kitchen shelves looking like colorful jewels, filled with preserved peaches, tomatoes, watermelon rind pickles, or even pickled okra (a favorite of only a few diners). Some restaurants even served Southern "sweet tea" in small Mason jars. But now there's a new use for these old jars—ecological lighting. A company has devised a small Mason jar with a solar-powered light inside. You can leave it outside to soak up the sun, then use it to light up the night on your patio or deck. This reminds me of how we used to collect lightning bugs in a Mason jar and watch them tickle our fancy by lighting up a warm summer night. Maybe that memory made someone think up this ingeniously ecological old/new idea.

Dear Lord, thank you for memories and ideas. Today's children have experienced so many technological "miracles." I wonder if they can still get as excited as we did, running across a lawn on a summer night, discovering that God made a little bug that can suddenly turn on its flashlight. Maybe they can. I hope so.

Never look down to test the ground before taking your next step:
Only he who keeps his eye fixed on the far horizon will find his right road.

Dag Hammarskjöld

I'm glad I'm not house-hunting right now. Scanning the classified ads, I see that condos are being marketed as the latest in environmental sustainability, with things like photovoltaic cells that generate solar power and an ultraviolet light that kills bacteria in the pool, reducing the need for chlorine. I don't even understand some of these "amenities." Photovoltaic cells? Am I the only old fogey who still stumbles over words like that? Luckily, these condos also feature recycled materials and antiques—and I can identify with them. My house is full of recycled garage sale "treasures" and a few real antiques, such as my great-grandmother's pitcher (painted with orange nasturtiums), my mother's chairs with carved "wing-like" tops (which a friend calls bizarre), and an old "writer's desk" I love. My house is environmentally sustainable— but I would sure like to get rid of those dust bunnies that recycle themselves the minute my back is turned.

Dear Lord, thank you for the memorable things our ancestors left to remind us to rejoice in the past. Before it's too late, please help today's generation work to save what is even more precious— not "things," but life-supporting necessities such as air and water. Fill us with respect for the "memorable things" you've left us which today need our help to be recycled and sustained. And don't let us forget that our stewardship is just as important as technical things like photovoltaic cells.

I need to put up with two or three caterpillars if I want to get to know the butterflies.

Antoine de Saint-Exupéry

My mother must have had a bridge that connected her with the good earth. She never had a fancy garden with prize-winning roses or exotic plants. Instead, she had a colorful patch of pass-along plants—a lovely variety grown from small plants friends had shared from their gardens or given her as gifts. Wherever she stuck a tiny slip in the earth, it grew and flourished. One of these pass-alongs was a Surprise Lily plant. It has a formal name but I think she got a kick out of its nickname—"the naked ladies." In late summer, the bare patch where the lily is planted puts forth a few naked stems which quickly grow two-feet tall and produce a cluster of pale, pink trumpet lilies atop those curiously leafless stems. My mother was always so tickled when the naked ladies bloomed overnight. She didn't care about the science of gardening. I think she just agreed with her friend who said, "I never put anything on my garden but coffee grounds and dishpans of dirty dishwater." Now that's science!

Dear Lord, maybe my garden doesn't grow as well as my mother's because, instead of a dishpan, I have an electric, automatic, push-a-button dishwasher! Yes Lord, I know I'm spoiled with all these labor-saving devices. Every day there are more and more doodads that electrically finish chores. Fortunately, I never can figure out how to use most of them, so I can often be ecologically correct thanks to my own ineptitude.

I love baked potatoes. They are so healthy, so good for you—unless you pile on butter, sour cream, and grated cheese. Of course, that's just the way I want them. However, I also have lots of wonderfully healthy potato recipes, and these appear regularly on our table. Recently I came across a brand-new potato idea. It seems that an old-time recipe for growing a healthy tree involved lining the planting hole with raw potatoes. The potatoes would hold in the moisture and, as they decayed, give nutrients to the young tree. With so many people planting trees today, this might be one of those old-time "grandma" recipes that is just as delicious today as it was then. Although young gardeners just might think this is a half-baked idea!

Dear Lord, I haven't planted many trees, but I've planted lots of flowers and bushes. Some flourished. Others did not. Maybe I should have asked a farmer for some planting secrets. Thank you for all the wonderful things you planted on our planet. Thank you for the old-timers who worked closely with the earth and had respect for your creations. Thank you for opening our eyes to the need to change our ways and become better stewards of the many blessings you have given us. And while I'm at it, thank you, Lord, for sour cream, butter, cheese and other delicacies that, when used in moderation, can dress up any dinner plate. For woman does not live by potato alone.

Don't believe everything you think.

Anon

Protect me, O Lord, for my boat is so small and your sea is so big.

Fisherman's Prayer

Oh, how I love to walk on a beach and feel the warm sand sift between my toes. I like to sit in a beach chair and watch the comings and goings of the waves, read or meditate or just get lulled into a lazy summer coma. The sand is always there, waiting for me to scrunch it and feel like a kid again. But you know what sand is? It's silicon. Forever the sand was always there, waiting for creative minds to figure out how to use it in computers, electronics, and countless technological innovations. You've probably heard all the jokes about how this huge industry grew up in Silicon Valley. Instead of scrunch *walking*, scrunch *thinking* turned lowly sand into devices that have literally changed the lifestyles of today. I am grateful for my computer and other electronics, but they never give me the warm, happy feeling of silicon between my toes.

Dear Lord, I looked up "silicon" in the dictionary and learned that sand is the most abundant element next to oxygen in the earth's crust. You sure made enough to go around, didn't you? Now it's up to us to preserve those sandy beaches, and to thank you for your generosity as we guard the grains of sand left in our planet's hourglass.

During the eleven years my Southern parents bravely lived in the alien territory of New York City, they were surprised by my unexpected arrival—which meant they now had a Yankee child. When I was five years old, they journeyed south again, so I grew up totally confused by my north/south heritage. My mother spoke longingly of her favorite New York spots and took me to tour them when I was a teenager. I thought of that trip today when I read news about the Empire State Building. Tourists go there for the spectacular view, but now birders go there in the spring and autumn to view thousands of migrating birds that fly at about the same height as the building's 86th floor observation deck. At night, some of the birds look like shooting stars soaring past. Some weary birds—like northern flickers or yellow-bellied sapsuckers, even land on the deck to rest. Often non-birders notice and ask questions about migratory patterns. Once people become aware, they care.

Dear Lord, when we hit New York, my migratory mother was like a shooting star, showing me the subway, shops, restaurants, sites and sights—and some days I felt like that yellow-bellied sapsucker, looking for a spot to rest. But I loved it. Lord, thanks for the vast variety of birds you made to decorate our environment. Thanks for the birders who not only watch birds but also watch out for them and protect them. And thanks for my loving, adventurous mother.

Though my friends tell me it's an interesting vacation destination, I have never visited the Rock in San Francisco Bay. I did see the movie, *The Birdman of Alcatraz*, and I think he might be surprised to know that this once notorious penal colony is now a tourist site…and a bird colony. From early spring to late summer, thousands of birds roost there during the breeding season. Though it was known as the "Island of the Pelicans" when the prison was built in 1934, human activity drove away most of the bird colonies. And since his research was done in Kansas before he came to Alcatraz, even the Birdman saw few birds there. But birds must think tourists are less scary than penal colonies, because today on the Rock you can see such seabirds as black-crowned night herons, snowy egrets, pigeon guillemots, cormorants, and gull chicks that look like big puffballs. If an abandoned prison with a scary history can turn into a happy nesting ground, full of life, surely there is hope for the rest of this planet.

Dear Lord, today I was in church, singing along, when we came to the line: "while to that rock I'm clinging." I started smiling, thinking of that big, bleak rock of Alcatraz and the birds cheerily clinging there while tourists come and go—and then we came to the last line of the song: "How can I keep from singing?" How indeed?

If necessity is the mother of invention, being a cheapskate is a close cousin. Cheapskating is about more than saving money. It's a challenge, a way to beat the system. And that can make it fun. Earlier generations lived through depressions and world wars and met the challenges with courage, creativity and humor. Sometimes solving problems had unexpected results. Our penny-pinching foremothers sewed together scraps of material to make warm bed covers. Today, quilting has become an art form. NASA had to invent items to use in a weightless atmosphere; many of those found their way into everyday life. Today we are threatened by warnings of desperate water shortages, non-degradable trash, carbon footprints, and other natural disasters. Now that more people are aware of the problem, we are finding new ways—even cheap ways—to solve these problems. And who knows how our inventions will change the world for the better?

Dear Lord, I'm thinking of this because, although I didn't have time, I had to go to the grocery today because my $10 coupon was only good today. Coping with a tight budget has shown me that being an inventive cheapskate can be fun. So thank you, Lord, for teaching me to see challenges as opportunities. And thank you for inventing people wiser than I will ever be who find ways to solve problems that may even save planets.

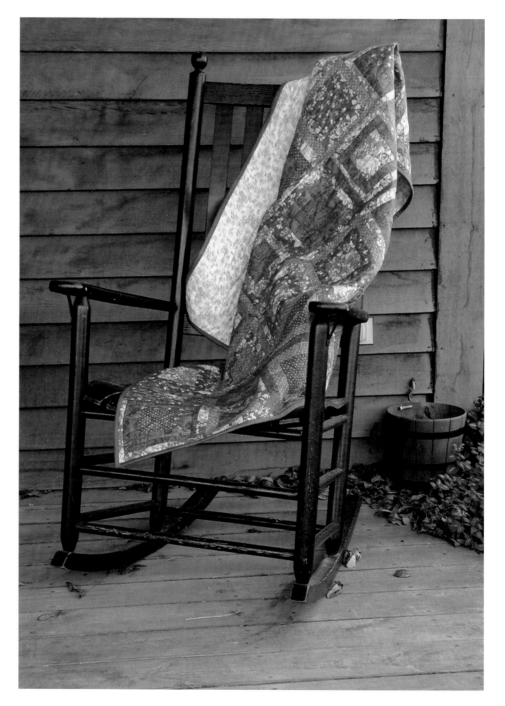

You can't roll up your sleeves if you're pointing your finger at somebody else.

Anon

Come forth into the light of things,
Let nature be your teacher.

William Wordsworth

There's a saying, "Age is just a number—and mine is unlisted." This applies to many busy, active senior citizens who, in "retirement," have recycled their lives into volunteer activities, travel, and even new careers. It doesn't matter how many birthdays they have celebrated. But in nature, age is often celebrated and carefully counted. There's a Methuselah tree, a bristlecone pine in the White Mountains of eastern California, thought to be the oldest tree in the world at about 4,760 years old. I don't know the age of the "General Sherman" tree in Sequoia National Park, but it's as tall as a 27-story building and its base is as wide as a three-lane highway. And if you walk through a Redwood forest in California and look up past the massive, tall trunks to the vaulting branches reaching for the sky, you might feel like you're in a cathedral—an old one that took a lot of years to build. Yes, age has its glories and stories—whether the numbers are counted or unlisted.

Dear Lord, a friend in her 90s told me she was so grateful God had let her live so long because it gave her the chance to learn so many lessons from the way other seniors handled age and infirmity. Help us all, Lord, to be wise enough to look beyond the challenges and learn lessons from our aging friends and aging planet.

What do American flags, zebras, football referees, and icebergs have in common? They all have stripes. The first three I have observed, but I never knew about the fourth until someone sent me an e-mail with beautiful pictures of Antarctic icebergs that wore stripes of many colors. How does this happen? When an iceberg falls into the sea, a layer of salty seawater can freeze to the underside. If this seawater is rich in algae, it can form a green stripe. Brown, black and yellow stripes are caused by sediment, picked up when the ice sheet grinds downhill toward the sea. And blue stripes are often created when a crevice in the ice sheet fills up with meltwater and freezes so quickly that no bubbles form. Again, God's creations come filled with surprises. And I guess you could say the same for American flags, zebras and referees.

Dear Lord, I love a parade with American flags, bands, and kids on the sidelines wearing funny or frilly sunhats, their expressions full of surprise and wonder. And the zebras at the zoo and the referees at the stadium are fun to watch, too. But I will probably never get to see a striped iceberg...except on my computer screen. Ain't technology grand! Thanks, Lord, for a world so full of surprises. Please help us keep it that way.

Historian Daniel Boorstin said, "Trying to plan for the future without a sense of the past is like trying to plant cut flowers." I don't think today's Americans would try to plant cut flowers, but it seems many of us are historically illiterate. Many of us have little knowledge of the past, with only a vague understanding of important events like the Civil War, the Great Depression, World War II, the atomic bomb, or man's first walk on the moon. To many of us, anything before we were born is "history" (said with a smirk). We have no interest in how our ancestors lived through difficult, dangerous times or survived by finding creative solutions that laid the groundwork for many advantages and opportunities we take for granted today. Hopefully, the current call to "save the planet" will spark our interest in how the past can teach us valuable lessons and inspire us to act.

Dear Lord, I confess. History was not my favorite subject either. Only when I married and started a family did I start to appreciate how amazing my parents were, how heroic my grandparents were, and how fascinating it can be to read about and learn from the past. Thank you, Lord, for the young people who are wiser than I was and who do appreciate the lessons of history. They are leading the charge to treasure the earth today, so that tomorrow's children can be proud of the history made by this generation.

Someone once said, "Curiosity is the wick in the candle of learning." Kids have been blessed with just such a wick. They ask, "Why is the grass green instead of orange?" "Why can't plants grow in caves?" "Why is it okay to eat green leaves like lettuce, but other green leaves are poison?" And of course, "Are we there yet?" Today, when the world is mechanized and computerized, most kids still have curiosity about the earth and how it works. This is why it's best to foster empathy in children, as well as an understanding of other people, animals, plants, and everything that makes our environment tick. *Sustainability* has been defined as, "Working to meet the needs of the present without compromising the ability of future generations to meet their own needs." With a little education, kids would just define it as an adventure.

Dear Lord, help us learn to think quickly so we can come up with answers to children's questions. Since we aren't there yet, help us ask questions ourselves so we can find new ways to do old things. Thank you for letting grownups have the opportunity to see the world through the eyes of children. Teach us about sustainability so the world will still be as wonder-filled when our children are grownups.

War is a terrible thing, bringing suffering, sacrifice, terror and loss. But there are different kinds of wars. Some bring out the best in people, resulting in unity and small or great victories. Recent floods have been fought by the National Guard, but also by strangers who voluntarily spent hours filling and stacking sandbags, trying to keep homes and cities safe when the levees broke. Fires, tornados, storms or even urban violence have, at times, brought people together to wage "war" in order to save their neighborhoods. In World War II, tires, gasoline, meat, metal and certain foods were scarce or rationed. But people endured because they felt they were saving the world with their efforts. Today, there are still terrible wars, but there is one global war we all can join—to save the beauty and the blessings of Earth for future generations. It's time to strike up the band and see if there will be enough volunteers to claim the victory.

Dear Lord, I've seen pictures of World War II: long lines for gasoline, ration books to buy certain items, and little boys pulling red wagons full of things for the scrap metal drive. They saved their world then and we can do it now—with your help.

HERB

DWARF

Did you ever hear of the word *potager*? In French, the word *potage* means "vegetable soup," so a *potager* is a vegetable garden—but not your out-the-back door vegetable garden. This type of garden is ornamental, year-round, and includes herbs and flowers in a structured design. A potager might be like a medieval monastic garden that not only provided food for the table, but also a location for meditation, prayer and food for thought. This brings back a memory from my youth: A friend and I visited her extended family in Holland. Her uncle took us to see a cousin who was a cloistered monk. He wore a long, white robe and a long, white beard. Women were not allowed there, but since we had come all the way from America, we were ushered into a private room—with a view of a potager—and were served delicious wine, cheese and bread the monks had made. Her uncle translated for us, but he would sometimes speak Dutch to us and English to her cousin, which led to lots of laughs and an unforgettable potager memory.

Dear Lord, pardon my French, but I hope there is still a potager here or there. Today, I'm enjoying my summer patio where I meditate and pray and revel in the beauty of flowers and trees and birdsong. I want it to stay this way forever, although I know autumn will come. The earth must have time to rest. But all winter I will look out and relive the memory of my own tiny garden, so unlike (and yet maybe just a bit like) the potager of my youth.

As a happy tourist in Rome, I was agog at the ancient sites and splendors, but I didn't think about the trees. If I went back today, I might be reminded that in 2007 Pope Benedict XVI thought enough about trees to get the attention of world leaders by announcing the Vatican would restore 37 acres of forest in Hungary that had been cut down in the Middle Ages. Why? Because the new forest will absorb enough carbon dioxide to offset all the pollution from the fossil fuel used to power Vatican City! This made the Vatican the first carbon-neutral state and offered a plan that could work quickly and inexpensively in larger areas. The Pope also announced the installation of solar panels to provide enough electricity to light, heat and cool the huge Paul VI Audience Hall, and he's encouraging the greening of Church operations around the world. Then, at World Youth Day 2008, Benedict urged youth to take the same discipline and care they use to collect cans, save fuel, etc. and apply that to their own private moral choices. He asked them to respect and revere all life, all God's creations. Growing trees, enthusiastic youth—what a hope-full combination.

Dear Lord, I've always loved trees for their beauty, shade and branches that provide nesting places for birds, but I never really thought of them as superheroes. Who knew they could be the ones to outdo Superman and Batman when the planet needed saving? You knew, didn't you, Lord? Thanks for trees—and youth.

Come, O God of my life, let my life grow green again in Thee,
put forth new flowers and regain the strength to bear its due fruit.

Saint Gertrude the Great

Nature is God's living, visible garment.

Johann W. Van Goethe

Dear Father, hear and bless
Thy beasts and singing birds,
And guard with tenderness
Small things that have no words.

Hurt no living thing;
Ladybird, nor butterfly,
Nor moth with dusty wing.
Nor cricket chirping cheerily,
Nor grasshopper so light of leap,
Nor dancing gnat, nor beetle fat,
Nor harmless worms that creep.

Christina Georgina Rossetti

To keep our planet balanced, we really need wetlands. But recently, with floods in our area, we have wished for less-wet lands. Thankfully, my home is not up a creek, or in an area near a levee that has given way, or on a river that has roared over its banks. But, just to remind me to have empathy and sympathy for others, my basement sprung a leak. We have had so much rain the ground is mushy, so I guess the water was just looking for somewhere to go—and it found our lower level. It was just in our laundry area. All the stuff I stored there was up on shelves, so I only had to mop. I would get it all mopped, sprayed with disinfectant, and dried up…and then it would rain again and my bucket and I would head back to the basement. Now we've had days of sunshine and roses, and our lower level is once again for laundry, not mopping. But it did make me more aware of the power of water and reminded me to pray for those whose lives were changed by too many wet lands.

Dear Lord, help us preserve the wetlands but also help those who have lost so much because of floods. Watching the television scenes of rushing waters, destroying homes and washing out roads and even concrete highways, reminds us to have more respect for something we so often take for granted. Your water can be such a blessing, and we can't live without it, but, like everything else, too much of a good thing can become a bad thing.

I asked for strength
and God gave me difficulties
to make me strong.

I asked for wisdom
and God gave me problems
to learn to solve.

I asked for prosperity
and God gave me a brain
and brawn to work.

I asked for courage
and God gave me dangers
to overcome.

I asked for love
and God gave me people
to help.

I asked for favors
and God gave me opportunities.

Anon

I'm afraid to look under my desk. There is a whole nest of black wires under there that remind me of a scene in the first Indiana Jones movie—a pit of writhing, hissing, you-know-whats. (I don't even want to say the word.) Most homes today have those nests of wires, connecting us to computers, printers, copiers, and phones—all necessary to our way of life. The modern world demands we stay connected, but that often takes up time we should (or wish we could) use for different kinds of connections—with nature, family, friends, and maybe even worthy causes. It can get lonely if you're not well-connected, but it is overwhelming when you get too connected. Like so much modern progress, it is sometimes the good news and the bad news.

Dear Lord, I read that sometimes aging computers are shipped from Europe or America to poorer regions of the world where the computer wires are burned and stripped to recover copper and other metals which can then be resold— another kind of recycling. Lord, my computer, like me, is aging, but so far we haven't been recycled, just plugged in—the computer to me and me to you. Thanks for that kind of connectedness.

Looking through the glass window of a hospital nursery at those tiny, innocent newborns is a Genesis moment, full of new beginnings and possibilities. In a much smaller way, plant nurseries are breathtaking, so full of new life. Recently I read about a tree nursery started by a non-profit camp. Students study the living organisms and ecosystems of that area. When the trees grow large enough, they are donated to schools so that other students can study reforestation. Also, some forests actually have their own nurseries with something called "nurse logs"—large logs covered with mosses and lichens. The not-too-dry, not-too-wet moss provides an ideal seedbed for tree saplings. One might see tall trees actually growing out of a fallen nurse log. Mother Nature at work again.

Dear Lord, you even taught trees how to nurture and recreate their own. Teach us how to nurse and cherish all your wonderful creations. You appointed us as stewards for the earth, but somewhere along the way we lost or ignored the instruction book and let things get out of hand. Now Lord, like fallen logs, we can start to nourish again. Thank you for always giving us a second chance.

We must live in the homes we make. That's why we have so many different kinds of houses. Birds can build a home out of anything, anywhere, but all creatures find a way to make shelters they can come home to. Although many homes in today's subdivisions seem to have a sameness about them, some people are turning to alternative building materials and reconfiguring designs using computer software. Some are building low-cost housing by recycling discarded materials like used tires and sheets of corrugated metal. Others are building energy-efficient homes that will offset any increase in construction cost by saving on maintenance and as much as 50 percent on utilities. By choosing carefully what we put into our houses and our lakes and the air we breathe, we will definitely impact our shared home—Earth.

Dear Lord, there are a lot of things we can't do a lot about, but we can change our own home. I guess it's the same with my prayer life. I've read books, gone to retreats, listened to homilies, and now I guess it's time for me to try some quiet time so I can recycle all those good ideas I brought home but just filed away. Help me, Lord, to choose carefully what I put into my house of prayer.

The international community needs to respect and encourage a "green culture."

Pope Benedict XVI, Rome, 2007

I've been fascinated with feathers ever since I saw photos of old-time movie stars wearing feather boas, or hats trimmed with elegant feathers. I just hope they gathered those feathers after our fine-feathered friends no longer had use for them, because birds do have many uses for feathers. Not only do they feather their own nests, some defend their nests from intruders by puffing out and bristling. Birds also fluff their plumage when the weather is cold to trap an insulating layer of air between their feathers and skin. Some even have a preening gland that produces oil to coat their feathers and weatherproof them. Of course, their most important use is the one we all envy—flight. Birds couldn't fly without feathers shaped to create an airfoil, which helps them rise and stay in flight. Humans have evidently recycled a lot of information from birds: We wear weatherproof jackets and travel in bird-like airplanes. We can also learn a lot from the resiliency of birds. They've had to adapt to the modern noises of cars, trains, factories, and yes, cell phones—and they still keep singing their sweet songs. Would that we do, too.

Dear Lord, in addition to noise, we've recently had to adapt to climate changes and new ways to recycle. We are more aware now of our wasteful lifestyles. It seems the phrase "It's for the birds" may not be an insult but a compliment. Lord, teach us resiliency and give us song.

All things bright and beautiful, All creatures, great and small,
All things wise and wonderful, The Lord God made them all....
He gave us eyes to see them, And lips that we might tell
How great is God Almighty, Who has made all things well.

Cecil F. Alexander

I heard about a lady who has many colorful, exotic plants in her garden. The most unusual of all is a small, hidden patch of hemlock. This carrot look-alike seems innocent enough, but it is a powerful, vertigo-inducing poison that can cause death. (I've read enough murder mystery books to know the power of hemlock potions.) She says she allows this dangerous weed to flourish because it has the capacity to draw rich minerals from the soil for compost. It seems even a poisonous plant can make a contribution to the earth. But I didn't believe this the year poison ivy decided to mix in with the honeysuckle on our back fence. I had to dress up like a space traveler—mask, gloves, enclosed in protective clothing—and try to pull it all out by the roots so the kids could play safely in the back yard. The only contribution it made was that it allowed my neighbors to enjoy watching my hostile attack on the alien space invaders.

Dear Lord, you know we have many poison patches in today's world, and they aren't all environmental. Traditional family values are being overgrown by the acceptance of undisciplined lifestyles, a media that applauds all broken commandments, and jokes about any spiritual approach to responsibility or respect for those who try to lead a good life. Help our society, Lord, to stop making such selfish (instead of selfless) contributions to the earth.

I never saw a Booby bird with feet of blue, dancing, showing off his feet for fun. I love the picture of a Booby Bird dancing to show off his blue-footedness, but I am not fleet-footed on a dance floor. That's why, with apologies to Gelett Burgess and her poem, "The Purple Cow," I really would "rather see than be one." These amazing birds hatch their chicks by wrapping their blue feet carefully around the eggs—and they even take turns. While one keeps the kids under wraps, the other flies off to find food and bring it back. They share. And who wouldn't admire someone who brings dinner home? The name may come from the Spanish word, *bobo*, which means "foolish fellow," because these high-flying marine birds are a bit clumsy walking on land, even though their feet are boo-tiful and blue. But they are definitely not foolish.

Dear Lord, I guess you know that the world needs fun things like birds with bright blue feet, so please watch over the boobys and don't let them become an endangered species. Please watch over all us human boobys too. We're all a bit clumsy at times—neglecting your earth instead of protecting it properly. Now it's become a problem we can't dance around. Sorry. So sorry.

Some of the books I keep stored in the basement are so old, they're beginning to take on a greenish tinge. And now some brand-new books are going green too. Recently, when a new edition of the *Shorter Oxford English Dictionary* came out, a lot of "green" was included in the 2,500 new words added since the 2002 edition. There's *carbon-neutral* and *emissions trading*, and a *carbon footprint* is defined as the amount of greenhouse gas emissions an individual is responsible for. A *green audit* inspects a company to define its impact on the environment. And *Chelsea tractor* is a British slang term for a gas-guzzling SUV. Words, words, words…they do define us. And they have such power now with our instant, interactive, intercontinental digital society. Type the wrong word and it can travel like wildfire before you can take it back. The same is sometimes true with friends and family—say the wrong word and instead of a carbon footprint, you leave a foot-in-the-mouth print. Whether using green words or familiar ones, the saying is still true: Be careful choosing words, because you may have to eat them tomorrow.

Dear Lord, my diet was already full of poorly-chosen words, and now I have to also be careful using environmental ones…or I may be charged with "greenwashing"—now a buzzword for misleading or false marketing claims. You know I tend to exaggerate when speaking before my mind is engaged, so help me, Lord, help me.

Our lives begin to end
the day we become silent about things that matter.

Dr. Martin Luther King, Jr.

Our town has lots of festivals and celebrations—Mardi Gras, St. Patrick's Day, the Fourth of July—and in recent years we've added Earth Day. It differs from the other holidays in several ways—no Styrofoam cups or containers; recycling bins set out for cans, bottles and cardboard; and used cooking oil that will be donated and recycled into fuel. There's music and art and entertainment, and lots of vendors and educational exhibitors, but also a "Peace Garden" for meditation, Tai Chi demonstrations, and an electronics site to recycle our old computers. And what about the food? Instead of hot dogs and nachos, there is a delicious variety of food and drink, all from local farmers and producers. Who comes to the Earth Day celebration? About 20,000 people came this year. Each year, nearly half of these are newbies coming to find out more about this greening thing. They come from all ages, backgrounds and neighborhoods. One of the organizers says, "We're not just preaching to the choir any more."

Dear Lord, Earth Day only comes once a year, but so does Mother's Day, so I guess we think it's okay to honor Mother Earth only once a year, too. Well, we don't really think that. We know we should honor mothers and fathers and Mother Earth and Our Father Who Art in Heaven every day. But at least an appointed day reminds us to revere (as well as celebrate) all year long.

Did you know that donkey harnesses in North Africa were involved in the discovery of penicillin? Dr. Ernest Duchesne, a young French army doctor, noticed Arab stable boys successfully treating saddle sores with a healing ointment made from the mold on damp saddles. He researched the mixture, and after using it to cure typhoid in guinea pigs, included the discovery in his doctoral thesis. Before he could pursue it further, however, he died of tuberculosis—a disease that this moldy ointment would some day help cure. Years later, the famous Sir Alexander Fleming received the Nobel Prize for his re-discovery of the healing, antibiotic effect of what became known as penicillin. Dr. Duchesne was posthumously honored as well. But the stable boys and the donkeys were never honored, although they knew about this cure for over a thousand years.

Dear Lord, I like this quote from Sir Fleming: "One sometimes finds what one is not looking for." I have often pursued foolish goals doggedly and then found something much more valuable that I was not seeking. Help us to seek and find proper solutions for our endangered earth. And thank you, Lord, for all the important discoveries like penicillin and all the small discoveries of your guidance and love that you send us in everyday life—even when we are not looking for them.

For several years now a popular fashion accessory has been a plastic bottle of water you carry with you wherever you go. It was supposed to be so healthy, so current—almost a status symbol. People purchased water from springs, glaciers, icebergs, Italian snow melt, and Tasmanian rain. But recently, a reaction to bottled water has flooded the media. University studies have shown that bottled water is not as pure as advertised, and some even has more bacteria than filtered tap water. And then there's the problem of all those plastic bottles piling up in the trash. One report stated that it takes 17 million barrels of oil a year just to make water bottles for the American market—enough oil to fuel 1.3 million cars for a year. Sounds like the status symbol of plastic hydration may soon stop being the status quo.

Dear Lord, I never could quite get why so many people were willing to pay big bucks for something we can find free at the kitchen sink. I can maybe understand the craze for endless redo-yourself programs, death-wish hobbies like mountain climbing or skate-boarding plus hula hoops, mood rings, or Paris fashions. But an industry selling status water? Well, I'm sure others can't understand many of my status-seeking fashion accessories. I guess you know we humans are always looking for ways to fill the void in our psyche—when all we have to do is look to you. Thanks, Lord, for always being there, our true status quo.

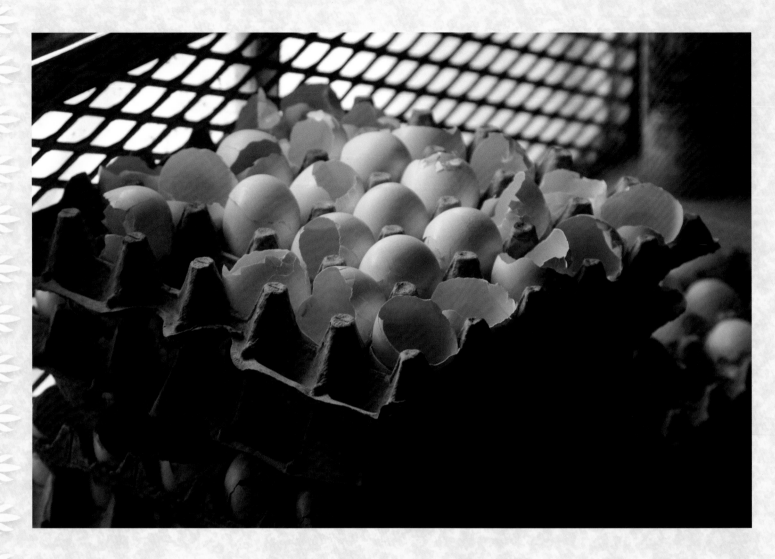

O Lord, how manifold are your works!
In wisdom you have made them all;
the earth is full of your creatures.

Psalm 104:24

My grandmother made biscuits every morning. Grandpa could not start his day without hot biscuits and strong, black coffee. Of course, Grandma added other goodies, such as homemade jellies and jams, fresh eggs from the chicken coop in the backyard, and sometimes even fried pork chops. My mother sometimes made biscuits, and often there were two kinds—the typical biscuits with crusty brown tops, and the "lily whites" that my Dad liked. I thought they had that name because she took them out of the oven while the tops were lily-white instead of brown. But maybe she called them that in honor of an age-old baking secret—White Lily All-Purpose Flour. If so, she never told me the secret, because I only recently heard about this flour that has been a tradition, used by generations of southern bakers to make weightless biscuits and cakes. Maybe that's why I never made biscuits. I sure ate lots of them, but mixing, rolling, cutting out, and baking them just right seemed too tricky for me to try. Now the silky White Lily Flour has become hard to find, so I guess I'll stick to my own age-old tradition: Biscuit? Don't risk it!

Dear Lord, I guess most of us would like to think we have led lily-white lives without a single evil spot on our souls or psyches. Unfortunately, most of us have, in one way or another, besmirched some area of our relationships, environment, neighborhood, planet or biscuit pans. But it's never too late to change. Just gotta risk it!

Chocoholics, workaholics, shopaholics—I have been one of them at different times and places. And now they tell me I am also a gasoholic. My car and I have been guzzling gas, running 'round town on unnecessary trips, and enjoying it. I love to drive down to the farmer's market to buy only a few things, so I'll have an excuse to come back soon. I love to drive to the lake and watch the water or the rowers or the sailboats float by. I drive to the hardware store for just one item, or to the book club without carpooling, or anywhere just to be out and about. Now, with gas prices and emission fumes bad for the budget and the environment, my car and I are going to have to stop meeting like this.

Dear Lord, when my son was young, I had lots of errands. When I took him someplace, I often said, "I just have to stop at the cleaners first. It will save me a trip." Or, "I just have to run into the grocery and get milk. It will save me a trip." One day, irritated at my stopping instead of going, he said, "Mom, you have saved enough trips for a trip around the world." Would that it were true, Lord. Would that it were true. Guess I gotta go back to saving trips. Who knows—maybe some day I will get that trip around the world.

Sometimes recycled ideas can be good too. My sister, probably remembering the goodies from our grandmother's garden, planted vegetables in her backyard at a time when it was not fashionable. It was such a treat to have summer supper at her house. She filled her freezer with just-picked goodies, and canned vegetables in Mason jars. Others are now recycling the idea of backyard gardens by filling vacant, inner-city lots with lush rows of crops (after getting permission from the land owners). Some even sell their produce at local farmers' markets. Families, neighbors, or even school classes share the responsibility and learn the joys of freshness.

Dear Lord, my sister had a green thumb, but I am just all thumbs. My vegetable garden proved that. Instead, I visit the local farmers' market and reward their hard work by buying armloads of freshness. In the same way, I wouldn't make it as a missionary, a doctor, a police or fire person, a contemplative nun, a mechanic, or a garbage truck driver. They all "recycle" in different ways, and I often benefit from their work. I always appreciate it. Thank you, Lord, for all the gifts you've given to the many different workers in your vineyard.

When the gas prices went up, people started talking about the need to cut back on driving—and put less gas emissions into the environment—by taking "stay-cations." They would use vacation time to stay home and visit nearby tourist spots. Some, remembering their less-scheduled childhoods, said, "We never took stay-cations. We took no-cations." Some wonderful memories come from those hazy, lazy days of summer when you didn't have to pack to go someplace just so you could take bigger and better photos than your friends and neighbors. Of course, travel is wonderful. It should be relaxing and fun and introduce you to new places and ideas. But maybe stay-cations will make folks more appreciative of their own hometown or their own backyard. Sometimes even an everyday problem like higher gas prices can send you in a new direction, where you might make memories in an old/new lo-cation.

Dear Lord, I love to travel both near and far. I like to be a tourist in my own hometown or travel as far, far away as my budget will allow. Whether in a big city or tiny town, I usually manage to peek into one or some of your churches, taking a few minutes away to drink in the quiet of the dark, empty pews, knowing that no church is empty when you are there. Realtors say the secret of their business is "location, location, location"—and, Lord, you have lots of great ones.

A friend is someone who dances with you in the sunlight
and walks beside you in the shadows!

Anon

"Y'all come back now." Southerners are often teased about their y'alls and other, friendly bits of colloquial language. My aunt would say, "I may be late for lunch, because I have to carry my friend home after church today." She always "carried" friends for a ride. Texans have their drawls, New Yorkers their crisp accents, and Bostonians their recognizable pronunciations. T-shirts in tourist shops bear Amish sayings like, "Ve grow too soon oldt und too late schmart." Or the German complaint, "The hurrieder I go the behinder I get." Or "Dutchy" talk such as, "Throw Father down the stairs his hat!" And of course, children have a language of their own. The way they put words together is cute, until we teach them "our" way. Love is the one language that should come naturally. As the song says, "You've got to be taught to hate." Today, as the world becomes smaller due to our technological ability to communicate instantly, maybe communicating the need to work together for the good of the planet will lessen our fear and hate and, as we get to know one another, maybe we can learn to speak the same language. Now that would be a miracle, wouldn't it? But I still believe in miracles.

Dear Lord, you and I know I have a language problem of my own—I can't stop talking! I'm always talking to you, Lord, and I'm sorry I seldom give you a turn. It's your turn now, Lord. I'm listening. Y'all come now.

One day I managed to trip over my own foot. I went airborne, landed on my right shoulder, and broke it. What a bummer. Couldn't I at least have been parasailing or skateboarding or something that would have made a good story? For a month, I had to do things "with one hand tied behind my back," although it was actually tied to my front. This was bad, but I also could not drive for three months. During this time, my husband ended up in the hospital twice. Then I heard a radio program on which a man spoke about the "power of helplessness." What? This man cared for helpless people and, by doing that, learned how we all depend on others in one way or another. Yes, I learned that lesson too. With no family nearby, I had to ask just about everybody I ever met to help with rides to the doctor, hospital, grocery and church. And it was a wonderful time. I found everyone eager to help, and even shared many laughs with them. Plus, I knew many people were praying for me. I truly believe that's why I healed quickly and happily.

Dear Lord, thank you for the helpers and the helpless. We need one another, especially now, when our planet is in trouble—so helpless without us to see and care for it. Teach us to be aware of others' needs and to be eager to share our time, talents, concerns, but also our laughter. A spoonful of sugar makes the medicine go down.

Many of life's failures are people who did not realize
how close they were to success when they gave up.

Thomas Edison

Did you ever wonder what a caterpillar thinks about? I never did until I heard about scientists who, as an experiment, exposed caterpillars to a noxious odor. If the caterpillars came near the odor, the scientists gave them an electric shock. Soon, the caterpillars learned to retreat from the odor before they were shocked. Then, as caterpillars will do, they went into hiding, changed their form completely, and did that amazing recycling miracle of turning into butterflies. Now the scientists introduced the noxious odor again and watched to see if the butterflies would remember. And sure enough, they did. Just like the caterpillars, they retreated, flying away instead of crawling from that shocking odor.

Dear Lord, I always thought that someday I just might recycle myself from a caterpillar into a social butterfly. That didn't happen. I just recycle cans, newspapers, and bottles. But I still have the hope and promise of turning into a new life form in eternity. And I sometimes have this niggling little question, wondering if—no matter how glorious my new life form might be—I will be able to remember any of the things that happened to me when I was a lowly human. Lord, I guess if you can make a butterfly remember, you can do the same for me. Of course, I know you can—but will you? I'm still wondering. And that's okay: It's great to live in wonder.

The faith waiting in the heart of a seed promises a miracle of life
which it cannot prove at once.

R. Tagore

Look deep into nature, and then you will understand everything better.

Albert Einstein

Birds make great sky circles of their freedom.
How do they learn that? They fall, and falling, they are given wings.

Rumi

The new catchphrase in the media is "carbon footprint." There have been others: In 2000, it was "hanging chads," and many years before that, during World War II, there was "Loose lips sink ships," a phrase that warned civilians not to talk about troop movements. Such phrases ask us to pay attention to the consequences of our actions. They call for a change of consciousness and conscience. Of course, it's easy for individuals and corporations and advertisers to repeat the catchphrase, but not so easy to overturn our old habits. Catchwords and phrases can manipulate us into thinking that saving the environment is already a reality, when we've only just begun to counter our energy-rich lifestyles and habitual over-consumption. Repeated too often, catchphrases become easy to ignore or make jokes about, instead of being an SOS to our consciousness and conscience.

Dear Lord, footprints I have seen—the muddy footprints my son tracked in on a just-mopped floor, when he came in from playing with his friends in our mud-box. (I had the bright idea to fill it with dirt instead of sand, thinking it would be easier to mop dirt than sift sand.) There are still the muddy prints I track in from gardening on a shoulda-been mopped floor. I can see those footprints. The carbon footprint, however, is still just an idea I have to work my brain around. Help us all, Lord, to see your footprints in our world. Let your footprints guide us to change our lifestyle and conscience.

Last year I gave a friend a T-shirt with the words, "Grill Sergeant!" emblazoned on the front. He was the designated grill master for his family, so it seemed appropriate. Many people in barbecue-intensive locations have designated grillers. And many more love the taste of grilled food—but some now feel it may be environmentally distasteful with all the smoky emissions. But never fear: Grilling will still be here. Someone has already come out with a redesigned grill that is ergonomic and friendlier to the atmosphere. And, as for charcoal, there is an all-natural charcoal on the market made from coconut shells. Along with a lot of my relatives and friends, I go nuts for southern bar-b-q, but I just found out about the coconut connection. I also never knew that grilling had anything to do with ergonomics.

Dear Lord, isn't it amazing how many things I know so little about? Of course, you and I do know that whenever I visit the relatives I must have some Tennessee barbecue. And when I'm there, although I didn't realize it before, all is ergonomically fine. (I know that now because I looked up "ergonomics" in the dictionary and learned that it is the science of designing and arranging things people use so that the people and things interact most efficiently and safely.) Yep, that's the way it is with my folks in Tennessee. Thank you, Lord, for relatives, grills and dictionaries.

A few years ago, my Dutch friend and I revisited Holland and were delighted to see picturesque old windmills. We went inside one, climbed to the top, and saw how energy efficient their machinery was in earlier times. That same day, while driving near the sea, we were surprised to see rows of very modern, trimmed-down windmills whirling to catch the sea winds. These were new to us then, but now it's estimated there are more than 97,000 large-scale wind turbines in some 60 countries. In Denmark, 20 percent of the country's electrical supply comes from wind and, on some days, it's 100 percent. The new-style, windy whirlers are not as pretty as the nostalgic Dutch windmills we visited, but they have zero CO2 emissions, no pollution, no waste, and quickly recoup the energy needed to build, operate and maintain them. Wind we always have with us—free, inexhaustible. Sounds like an idea that's not just full of hot air.

Dear Lord, I just learned that one of the largest wind turbines is in Hawaii. Since I have already "researched" the ones in Holland, it seems logical that I should now check out those in Hawaii. So far, my suggestion to add that to the family budget has been met with a free and inexhaustible hot-air response that was not energy efficient. Oh well, your wonderful wind still visits my patio, and I love it. Thanks.

This morning I looked out my kitchen window and saw above my neighbors' house a small, dark, angry gang of clouds clustered around the sun like a band of ragamuffin bandits, pushing the sun back, threatening it, allowing only a glimpse of light to peek out. As I watched, I knew it was an echo of my morning. In spite of many blessings in my life that past week, there I was, coffee cup in hand, letting my personal, dirty-little-bandit doubts and regrets cloud my head, telling me to find an excuse to "mislay" my to-do list and concentrate on my worry list. Fortunately, the sky is as unpredictable as a woman trying on shoes. Within minutes, the sun pushed its way through the cowardly blackguards who dashed away in defeat, while the sun went about its to-do list of filling my backyard and kitchen window with golden splashes of hope and encouragement.

Dear Lord, I guess I better dash away and get my recyclables to the curb before pickup, dash back in to wash some non-recyclable pots in my kitchen, and decide which to-do I should tackle first—right after I get a second cup of coffee and take a 10-minute time out to just sit in your sunshine and welcome you into my morning and my much-blessed world and feel oh-so grateful.

There is a sixth sense, the natural religious sense, the sense of wonder.

D. H. Lawrence

There's a famous book titled *A Wrinkle in Time* that presents the possibility of time travel. I think about that book when I look in the mirror and see the wrinkles caused by my own travel through time. I've grown accustomed to my face, but if I had the cash, I might be able to travel back through time by using some of the many wrinkle-removing potions for sale today. Some have even jumped on the green bandwagon. Their "all natural" promise to change the environment of your face seems a bit frivolous, but at least it shows that more and more people are giving at least a nod to our global problem. To some of us, the idea of changing our lifestyle to be environmentally correct is so overwhelming, it does not compute. But taking one small step can lead to more. We can't travel back in time, but we can travel forward, one step at a time—even with just a new wrinkle in wrinkle cream.

Dear Lord, can you imagine that I would even talk to you about something as frivolous as wrinkle cream? I guess you are not surprised, because you already know how silly I can be—and you did give me that frivolous gene. Okay. I'll get back to work, meditating while I do this morning's dishes and later when I pull weeds in the garden. But Lord, do you realize how dangerous that is, as dishwater and sunshine both make my hands and face wrinkle?

I was sitting on the patio, quietly reading, when the thunder began. It roared, it rumbled, it reverberated…I loved it. Thunder always reminds me of God's majesty, might, power and unpredictability. I know it can signal danger, but there was no lightning in sight, so I wanted to stay where I was, listening to God's voice, savoring the beauty of the flowers and trees until the first rain drops started. Yes, I know there are meteorological explanations for thunder, but I like mine, as well as the ones children invent. "God is bowling." "The angels are playing war games, shooting off cannons." "Jesus has a new sports car and is revving up the motor." Anyway, the big black clouds slowly moved away, the thunder faded, and the predicted storm didn't come. The sun appeared, shining happily. It was like so many of the thunderous moments of my life, the predicted storms that I spent valuable time worrying about—before the sun came out and put me to shame.

Dear Lord, thank you for giving us forgetful folks both practical and spiritual reminders. Maybe your thundering today was to tell me I had been reading my mystery novel long enough and needed to get off the patio and put out the recycling for tomorrow's early-morning pickup. I did do that. But I think you also wanted to remind me of your majesty, might, power and unpredictability. I got the message.

Time to have a *savasana*. I just learned this is the name for the relaxing posture one uses before and after yoga. It's supposed to ease the mind, body and spirit. Since it does not involve any bends, lunges or pretzel poses, I think I could manage it. I know yoga works wonders for many, but today I'd like to leave that out and go right to the before-and-after…for a double *savasana*. With so many things to worry about today—natural disasters, terrorism, the economy, and yes, the environment—we all need to take timeouts to put away the negatives for a while. Instead of grousing about the news of the day, griping about the extra trouble it takes to recycle, grumbling about the high prices at the grocery store, how about trying to un-whine while we unwind? Sure, there are lots of reasons to be troubled, and it's important to do what we can, in our own little way, to try to correct problems, but dwelling on only the negative is like hopping on one foot—it can make us lose our balance. So today I will put both feet up, breathe in, imagine a balance sheet that lists all the good things in my life, and have a *savasana*.

Dear Lord, I was listening to a golden-oldie album and one song suggested we should "Accentuate the positive, eliminate the negative, latch on to the affirmative, and don't mess with mister-in-between." Help me do that, Lord, even for just a few minutes each day, and maybe it will lead to a more balanced life, mixing stress with "savasanas" plus lots of thanksgivings.

In this little hazelnut I saw three properties. The first is that God made it,
the second is that God loves it, the third is that God preserves it.
But what is that to me? It is that God is the Creator and the Lover and the Protector.

Blessed Julian of Norwich

Dogs and cats hate them. Sometimes they wake the baby and make him cry. But reefs like them a lot. For years, vacuums have been cleaning our carpets and now they may be the answer to saving reefs along the Hawaiian coasts. When a fast-growing algae was overwhelming the reefs, almost smothering them, marine biologists tried a new idea. They began to dive below the surface with a giant vacuum hose that snaked up to a pump on a barge. Named the Super Sucker, the machine has no blades, so it can remove the algae without killing crabs, sea cucumbers, or other small creatures. And it seems to be working. For a different reason, Caribbean coral reefs—which have been called rainforests of the ocean—are also in danger. They are rapidly declining because of climatic change that results in warmer, more acidic water which is very damaging to coral. But there too, conservationists are working to save these complex, biologically-diverse ecosystems that anchor a strong web of life in the ocean. Hopefully, they too will find a Super Solution.

Dear Lord, like the algae, stuff seems to accumulate in my house, overwhelming my idea of tidiness and smothering my passion for vacuuming. I don't guess I could find a subdivision-sized Super Sucker when it's time to shovel out some unnecessary stuff in my house and head? That might give me more time to pray for those who are working hard to save your underwater marvels and the rest of your troubled planet. Bless them, Lord. And thank you.

Lobster and champagne, steak with all the trimmings, and fancy ooh-la-la French concoctions all have their place in the food chain. But sometimes, nothing will quite do except a burger and fries. They say Americans have a love affair with fried food, and who am I to contradict? But now it seems there might be an environmental bright side to deep-fried. It was reported that 4.5 billion gallons of fry oil left annually from our greasy goodies could cleanly power more than 10 percent of the nation's diesel engines—more than 528,000 cars—for a year. In 2007, a United Kingdom fast-food chain announced their 155 delivery trucks would switch to running on recycled vegetable oil collected from their chain's 900 restaurants. On a smaller scale, an American engineer drove cross-country in his fry-oil powered car and said making his own fuel was simple and cost only about $1.00 per gallon. You can also buy biodiesel commercially, which would be even simpler. Making your own fried hamburger? Maybe. Making your own fry-oil fuel? Maybe not.

Dear Lord, I don't think my car can digest fry fuel yet, but it sure sounds like a good idea. In the meantime, Lord, do you think I can do my bit for the environment by buying more fast food so there will be more leftover fry oil? Maybe... maybe not.

As I am always trying to keep my errant hairdo from that gone-with-the-wind look, today I bought something called "styling putty," hoping to putty my "do" into some kind of style. But when I read the label, one ingredient listed was "horsetail." This got my attention. I've never been up-close-and-personal with a horse. Should I really put a horse's tail on my head? Actually, it turns out that horsetail doesn't come from a horse but is a non-flowering herb that can grow up to two-feet tall. This plant is thought to have been around since the days of the dinosaurs, and it seems Native American tribes once used horsetail to treat certain ailments. This plant is so rich in amino acids and minerals, it is supposed to strengthen my fingernails as well as perk up my hairdo. What an herb! What a tale of a tail.

Dear Lord, how exciting to meet a plant sturdy enough to survive the trampling of dinosaur feet and the dangers and insults of the planet through the centuries. Yet if I had found it in my tiny garden, I would have probably torn it out, mistaking it for a pesky weed, never knowing its history or the many ways it has been useful for everything from Native American ointments to today's hairdos. Help me Lord, in the future, to be less quick to judge those pesky-seeming plants, as well as those pesky-seeming people who might actually be real heroes in our race for survival as a species.

"Hope" is the thing with feathers—
that perches in the soul—
And sings the tune without the words—
And never stops—at all—

Emily Dickinson

Today I went to the mailbox and, as usual, it was full of bills and catalogues. There was a time when I would find a friend's letter, or a crayoned greeting from a younger friend, or even a BW (before wedding) love letter from my fiancé! Today, any important announcement or greeting comes in the form of an e-mail that is instant and nice—but so easily erased. Even if you save them, new computers will keep coming out that can't read old, saved e-mails. Future generations will not find packets of old letters wrapped in blue ribbons. They won't be able to read about all the things that threatened this generation: firsthand stories of high prices for fuel and food, people losing their homes or jobs because of companies downsizing, natural resources being exploited. But they also won't read about how so many around the world saw the danger and worked together—as families, as friends—to become good stewards of their home planet.

Dear Lord, I was clearing out a file and came across an old letter that told about a relative making his First Communion, wanting a white prayer book with a picture of Jesus in a red bathrobe, and how I found one for him. That relative now has grandchildren making their First Communions. Both he and I had forgotten the story until the letter brought it back. Emily Dickinson said, "A letter always seemed to me…like immortality." Even if they don't have letters, I hope future generations will hear about today's troubles, but only as problems we prayed about and were able to solve.

When you build a house, it stays the same until you need to renovate. A garden is different. Flowers, like children, change every year—and you can't ignore them. One year your garden looks perfect, and you plan to keep it that way forever and never change a thing. The next year a plant that always flourished starts looking puny and needs extra attention, while one that lived quietly in its own little corner suddenly grows rampant and heads in a new direction. Plants have a life of their own. You try everything—new plant food, more water, less water, more sun, less sun. You transplant, talk nicely or harshly to them every day, and beg them to return to their former glory. Sometimes they listen, sometimes they don't. A garden can take a lot of time and digging. It can complicate and challenge your life, but it keeps you on your toes and on your knees, praying for help. But an environment without gardens and children and surprises would be empty and boring. That's the beauty of it all.

Dear Lord, to remind me of that beauty, I have a plaque on my kitchen wall with this quote from Kipling: "Oh Adam was a gardener…and God who made him sees… that half a gardener's work is done upon his knees. When your work is finished…you can wash your hands and pray…for the glory of the garden that it may not pass away." Thanks to Kipling, and to you, Lord, for reminding me to always wash my hands and pray.

Perhaps reluctantly we come to acknowledge that there are also scars
which mark the surface of our Earth: erosion, deforestation,
the squandering of the world's mineral and ocean resources
in order to fuel an insatiable consumption.

Pope Benedict XVI

I've found a plant that, like my lopsided pine tree, offers inspiration. It's called the Resurrection Fern. During a dry season, it rolls itself into a ball and plays dead. But as soon as it gets some moisture, it wakes up and grows green again. You can even watch this magic trick indoors by planting one in a six-inch pot. If you stop watering it, it "dies." When you water it again, it comes back to life. This is not a very attractive plant, but it's a good one to have if you sometimes forget or neglect to water your plants—or if you sometimes need inspiration. I myself am not very attractive on days when I'm overwhelmed with a long to-do list. I might neglect some duties, forget others, and groan and moan and feel sorry for poor-overworked-me all the while. It takes more than a drink of water to bring me back to life, but a candy bar and a prayer, and the thought of the Resurrection Fern, usually does the trick.

Dear Lord, I guess most people need steady care and watering to survive today's busy whirl. We also need reminders to stay on the course, to be good stewards. A recent poll reported that only one in five Americans felt they could "make a difference" when it came to the environment. But things are changing as more and more begin to recognize the value of greening the earth and greening their attitude. Thank you, Lord, for lessons like the magic of the Resurrection Fern, to remind us of the hope of resurrection.

When my son was in grade school, he brought home a turtle that would look really ugly to someone who didn't like reptiles, but that probably would look beautiful to another turtle. He was a fine specimen, and we have pictures to prove it. One day, he got tired of us and crawled away from home, but I still wonder sometimes where he went. I just read about a much larger leatherback turtle who swam for nearly 650 days and over 12,000 miles (from New Guinea to the coast of Oregon) to feast on her favorite jellyfish. How do we know this? Well, a transmitter attached with a flexible harness (which evidently did not get in the way of her swimming) enabled researchers to track the turtle's trip. After the feast, the turtle left Oregon and headed for the tropical waters southeast of Hawaii, before the battery in her custom-fitted, transmitter backpack gave out. And it was about time. The researchers are studying migrations to identify waters where they may need to conserve turtle populations. But a girl has to have her privacy—especially after a jellyfish feast!

Dear Lord, I hope the researchers learned a lot from that Olympic swimmer's trip. She sure set an example for us all. The next time I get discouraged about a goal of mine, remind me, Lord, of the lesson of the turtle. No matter how far you need to go to reach your goal, you gotta keep swimming.

A friend visited Egypt, the Pyramids, and all the ancient wonders, and came home and put together a beautiful slide show. I loved watching it and experiencing that amazing land, albeit secondhand. Since then, I've been interested in the debates about how those pyramids were built 5,000 years ago with only manpower and copper tools. Now, it seems there is evidence that might finally solve the mystery. In two pyramids in Giza, a team of scientists examined samples of local limestone with electron microscopes and analyzed the samples chemically. They concluded that the Great Pyramids were not built of limestone blocks but of concrete casts. Concrete made by mixing limestone particles with a silica-rich binder could have easily been transported and poured in casts on-site. If confirmed, Egyptian builders will get credit for inventing concrete. Even better, their formula may provide a clean, inexpensive, long-lasting substitute for the kind of cement widely used today, which is highly polluting. Another lesson from ancient Egypt!

Dear Lord, isn't it strange how we always want to do something newer and better, but sometimes we just have to look to the past to find solutions for the present? Of course, we do have lots of newer and better inventions and discoveries (like those electron microscopes they used on the Pyramids), and we even have newer and maybe better ways to pray. But I still like the old one-on-one conversation, don't you?

Summer's lease hath all too short a date.

William Shakespeare

I'm always so happy to get a phone call from my favorite nephew. He fills me in on all the family news from Tennessee. But yesterday I could hardly hear what he was saying because of the background noise. I finally asked, "Are there frogs living in your house now?" He laughed and explained that he was sitting outside by the pond. He had installed the pond in his backyard since the last time I visited. He said as soon as he had dug the pond, an extended family of frogs moved in. While we were talking about family affairs, they evidently were too.

Dear Lord, just the thought of a pond full of chatty frogs makes me think of lazy, hazy summer days—time to withdraw from the daily clutter, to rest and renew. Today's increasingly exhausting, busy way of life leads some to anxiety, fear and even depression. But an occasional pond and a prayer might be just what we need to become grounded again. Robert Frost once said, "I'd like to get away from earth for a while—and then come back and begin again." Dear Lord, remind me and my generation to take timeouts to breathe easier. Remind us to begin again, to rejoice in your gifts, your love and your presence—before our busy schedules make us croak.

Would you believe there's a little animal called a marmot who could cough you to death? Believe it or not, these little animals that live in Mongolia are susceptible to a lung infection known as the bubonic plague—yes, the Black Death! And when they cough, they can infect fleas, rats, and ultimately, people. But they do have nice relatives. One of their cousins is a benign, pot-bellied member of the squirrel family who squeaks but does not cough. Another is the groundhog that only scares people once a year by coming out of a hole on February 2 to predict another six weeks of bad weather. (Well, all families have a few difficult relatives.) Of course, the plague is not a laughing matter, but if you're ever on the Mongolian steppe and see a little marmot-looking animal coming toward you, go the other way.

Dear Lord, we probably don't have to worry too much about marmots, but we do have lots of plagues in society that should scare us enough to make us want to work at erasing them. You know what they are, Lord—immorality, selfishness, materialism and, only recently acknowledged, our total disregard for protecting the planet you created for us. Forgive us, Lord, for not noticing what is happening to our world. Guide us in the right ways, to cherish and honor and save your creations. It really is not a laughing matter.

When my son was barely a toddler, we moved from an apartment into a house with a nice, fenced-in backyard. He loved his new playground. One day, I looked out the kitchen window and all was quiet—none of the usual neighborhood sounds, only a gentle breeze. My son sat in the grass, looking into the distance—or maybe into the future. He seemed to be drinking in the quiet. Whenever I get nostalgic about those baby days, that picture floats into my mind. I compare it with today, when there is hardly ever any real quiet. With cell phones, iPods, chat rooms, video games, television, and radio (just to name a few of our everyday distractions), we are saturated with noise. The media owns our attention from babyhood through senility. Too much of a good thing can be waaaaay too much. Unfortunately, that may be true of some who are using environmentalism to jump on the greening bandwagon with media ads, sales, and one-time-only attention grabbers. Too much hoopla may make this call to action seem like a fad and turn off the very people who need to hear it.

Dear Lord, help us be wise enough to see the difference between the workers and the noisemakers. Help us to remember the story of the little boy who cried wolf, so we won't wait too long until we are alerted to the real danger.

Labor to keep alive in your breast that spark of celestial fire called conscience.

George Washington

What an exciting morning. I took a trip in a time machine. I visited the past by touring a Victorian home built in 1885. But I also visited the future, because this house had been updated to be totally earth-wise. Kitchen appliances were powered by solar panels. The insulation was cellulose made from recycled newspapers. And instead of tile, the owners installed eco-friendly cork floors. Disposing of fruit and vegetables in a "can of worms" made great compost, and even the lovely, winding garden path was edged with native plants that required little watering or maintenance. But just in case, there was an old-time rain barrel. Every nook and cranny surprised me with clever ways to transform yesterday into tomorrow. I found that looking back while looking forward can be quite a head-turning experience.

Dear Lord, what a great lesson: Honor the past, look to the future, live in the present. The volunteers who conducted the tours were a combination of young and old, but all were totally enthusiastic about their accomplishments and eager to share ideas and suggestions with others interested in following their example. Thanks, Lord, for tour guides, tour takers, and ready-to-learners. And thanks for the fun time-machine trip.

My husband has always liked to read British mysteries and histories. We were even able to visit Merry Olde England… twice. Each time was a treasure to remember. But once, setting out to visit Kensington Gardens, we became sidetracked and never made it. So we never saw the sparrows. The gardens were once home to thousands of sparrows (as was much of Europe). The birds were content with people-places. They nested under the eaves of buildings and ate the crumbs of city streets and rural villages. But a few years ago, changes in agricultural practices meant fewer seeds and weeds. Rural sparrows began disappearing. Soon, city birds did too. A 1925 survey counted 2,603 sparrows in Kensington Gardens; a year 2000 survey found only eight. Conservationists fear that more pavement and less greenery left too little food for the sparrows to feed their nestlings. It's too late now for us to go back to London and see the sparrows, but we still see a few in our hometown. We must still have enough seeds, weeds and insects in the United States. Good news, bad news.

Dear Lord, sparrows were so common we thought they would always be with us. But like so many other common things, we didn't appreciate them until they began to disappear from our lives. Help us, Lord, to notice everyday joys that we have now, and appreciate them before they are lost.

I did not read books the first summer; I hoed beans. Nay, I often did better than this.
There were times when I could not afford to sacrifice the bloom of the present moment
to any work, whether of the head or hands.

Henry David Thoreau

I never thought I would be jealous of an albatross. I knew this was the name of a bird, but in my head an albatross was something unpleasant that hung over you. I don't know where I got that idea, unless it was a dictionary definition, which mentions an albatross as something that causes "persistent deep concern or anxiety." I also don't know why, in the last few years, albatrosses have been tracked by earth-orbiting satellites. But you know what? Results showed that a fifty-year-old albatross will have flown over three million miles, covering distances equal to flying around Earth at the equator three times every year. They live long and fly far and because of this they contend with almost every effect people exert on the sea. Everything we do to the oceans, albatrosses feel. So I could be jealous of the albatross, because I would love to spend time by the sea, flying hither and yon. But with today's polluted waters, it could definitely cause "persistent deep concern or anxiety." So sad.

Dear Lord, I've done my share of sitting by the sea and flying hither and yon—always tourist class, of course. Maybe thinking about this bird and its endless journeys as it contends with the changing oceans will remind me not to be jealous but rather teach me about persistence in preserving the oceans.

Are you suffering from video-mania? Have you become so fascinated with the Internet, videogames, podcasts, text messages, DVDs, and PDAs that you forget to look out the window? There's a fascinating world out there waiting to entertain you. Maybe you have not been infected with this new cultural disease, but someone you know is suffering from it right now. Not long ago, one of the most popular forms of entertainment was having a one-on-one with nature—a walk in the park, a picnic, a canoe ride, a hike in the woods, a trip to a lake or the ocean or the mountains, or maybe just planting a garden in your own backyard. In the last few years, however, people in "civilized" areas have become more prone to electronic recreation. Seeing nature on TV can be wonderful, but a televised viewing of the Grand Canyon, a spectacular sunset, or even a flower garden is not the same as being there.

Dear Lord, forgive us for settling for electronic indoor appliances and neglecting your great outdoors. One-on-ones with nature can be such fun—for both adults and children. Getting outside more often will make us all more conscious of the need to protect and cherish our planet. We need the real thing—not a video of the real thing.

Tom Sawyer had a bright idea, but it just didn't work in my circle of friends. The little fence around my patio needed rehab. I got together stain, brushes, and a drop cloth, and on a nice, sunny morning went out and started painting. I didn't get far before it was time to clean up, change clothes, and go to my monthly book club. Once there, I said, "I had so much fun this morning painting a fence. Would some of you like to come home with me today and help finish it?" The ladies hooted and said, "We read the book!" So I paid a handyman to finish the fence (and when he thought I wasn't looking, he redid the spots I had started). The next day I heard on the radio about a group that recycles leftover paint by mixing together cool or warm colors, then adding a bit of white (or whatever color is needed) to make each gallon bucket a pleasant shade. They send the paint to Peace Corps volunteers, who take the buckets to remote villages to paint schools, houses, and other municipal structures. What a bright idea!

Dear Lord, as usual, I was only half-listening, so I didn't catch the name of the group that's doing this, but you probably know who they are, so would you please bless them and help them in this project? Actually this is a perfect example of recycling. I think I'll recommend it to my book club.

Nature and God—I neither knew
Yet Both so well knew me
They startled, like Executors
Of my identity.

Emily Dickinson

When I was a preschooler and my sister was a teenager, our family moved to a different house. It had a living room fireplace, and my sister thought it would be fun to build a fire—so she did. My father was on his way home when a fire engine screeched past him. He followed, not knowing they were both going to the same place—our new home. The little fire caused by sparks shooting out of the dirty chimney was quickly doused, but the whole thing was exciting for a preschooler. I sometimes think of that day when I hear a siren and see a fire engine whisk by. Sirens, alarm clocks, and even signs or labels ("Beware!" "Poison!") do get our attention and bestir a sense of urgency. Today, there are a lot of labels advertising "energy-saving"; "super-organic"; "Earth-loving"; and other attention-grabbers. Instead of helping green up America, some are only an attempt to get our greenbacks. So it's wise to be alert and pay attention to warnings—but don't be fooled by false-alarm siren songs.

Dear Lord, when I was a little older than a preschooler, a teacher told us that whenever you hear a siren you should say a quick little prayer for whomever needs help—and for the people who are on the way to help them. I've never forgotten that, and today maybe that's one thing everybody can do—pay attention to the alarm and say a prayer for our planet.

For years now, we've heard all about *lo-cal* food and how good it is for us. Now we have new instructions: We are to eat *local* food, which means food grown locally (or at least nearby) so we don't have to worry about the fuel it took to transport it from a farm to our dinner table. In recognition of international food shortages, a growing movement of "locavores" is encouraging us to think global, eat local. And the very best local is in your own backyard, if you can manage it. To set an example, Woodrow Wilson installed a Liberty Garden and watched sheep grazing on the White House lawn. And in World War II, 40 percent of the nation's produce came from citizen gardeners. It sounds so independent, so American, to feed your own by growing your own.

Dear Lord, this is one idea we don't have to run up the flagpole to see if anybody salutes. In times of crises, Americans have always gone to extra trouble to "do what is right." I hope we haven't gotten too stuck to our easy chairs to rally 'round this time and either grow or shop locally. Remind us, Lord, to truly think global, eat local.

EPILOGUE

In conclusion, an explanation….

When I had lunch with the grasshopper and set out to write this book, I was not very eco-savvy. I knew a little (but not enough) about the immediate need for stewardship on behalf of today's changing earth. I didn't realize there were so many places where our planet is threatened and so many surprising ways in which that threat touches our lives.

I had even less information about all the good news. I kept coming across stories and statistics—from reliable sources—about the ways people are working to solve today's earthly problems. That's why we should focus not on what has been lost but on what remains—and needs to be cherished and saved.

Hopefully we all have a bit of the child left in us, the yearning to wander and explore the unknown, to discover and achieve something—to forge ahead and change the world. Most of us won't be able to do something big, but we can each make an impact. Today, we are invited to reestablish our sacred connection to the earth just by doing small things, just by being aware.

That's why I have taken the humorous approach regarding our journey to save the planet. Life is a gift to be enjoyed and appreciated. So let us be joyful as we join this new endeavor of stewardship. Let us rediscover all the beauty of God's creations and revere them—and in the process maybe even learn to see eternity in a grain of sand.

The great thing in this world
is not so much where we are,
but in what direction we are moving.

Oliver Wendell Holmes

Achieving starts with believing.

Anon